# ROYAL DENVER
# GIBSON
## A TWENTIETH CENTURY APOSTLE

By

NARA GIBSON WENRICH

Intermedia Publishing Group

## ROYAL DENVER GIBSON
### A TWENTIETH CENTURY APOSTLE

Published by:
Intermedia Publishing, Inc.
P.O. Box 2825
Peoria, Arizona 85380
www.intermediapub.com

ISBN 978-1-937654-20-7

Unless otherwise indicated, all Scripture quotations are taken from the King James Version of the Bible.

Scripture quotations taken from the New King James Version. Copyright © 1982 by Thomas Nelson, Inc. Used by permission. All rights reserved.

Additional copies of this book are available by mail. Send $12.99 each (includes tax and postage) to:

**Nara Gibson Wenrich**
**4063 Seabury Dr.,**
**Dallas, TX 75287**

For copies of the "Prayer of Dedication" on CD write to
The Pentecostals of Alexandria
2817 Rapids Ave.
Alexandria, LA 71301

# CONTENTS

# DEDICATION

This book is dedicated to the descendants of Royal Denver and Eulah Annie Gibson; whether living, or, are yet to be born.

The decades of prayers that were prayed on your behalf are yours to claim and to possess. The blessings and benefits stemming from their righteous lives will follow you like a shadow throughout your lives and the lives of your children.

The book is also dedicated to the spiritual sons and daughters of Roy and Eulah Gibson. You entered the Kingdom of God through their powerful ministry and they mentored you, established you, and planted you firmly and solidly in the courts of the Lord.

May all who read this book be blessed, encouraged, and inspired to be all that God designed, purposed, and intended for you to be.

> *"Go now, write it on a tablet for them, inscribe it on a scroll, that for the days to come it may be an everlasting witness." Isaiah 30:8*

# ACKNOWLEDGMENTS

My sincere and heartfelt thanks to LaVerne Gilbert Gibbs who untiringly guided me through the long, often tedious process of getting this book published. I also want to thank her wonderful husband, Mickey, who kept my house intact, my car running, and my flowers flourishing through his expertise and two soaker hoses.

Many thanks to everyone along the way who encouraged me, prodded me, and prayed for me during the inception, continuance, and completion of this project. I especially want to thank those who contributed their stories that are included in this book.

Special thanks to my sister, Vesta Mangun, for praying for me; and her encouraging words throughout the process of this writing. The transcription by Mary Wolfe of our father's dedicatory prayer from the CD archives was an enormous contribution. Thank you, Vesta, for arranging it and thanks to Mary Wolfe for doing the hard work.

Thanks to Phil Jones for so graciously permitting me to use his beautiful, inspiring words that he wrote for "Popsey" Gibson's funeral service program. The words captured so succinctly the essence of my father's long, productive life.

Lastly, I thank God for giving me the strength, the courage and the ability to recall from my mental archives the deeds and accomplishments that are recorded in this factual account.

The Author

# PREFACE

Like Goliath's sword, there was never—and will never be—a man quite like R.D. Gibson.

R.D. Gibson had a voice that when lifted in prayer could open heaven and cause hell and its demons to tremble. He had unwavering faith and a commitment to the gospel of Jesus Christ that allowed no room for challenge or compromise. He was a man of prayer and a man of the Word. He was an anointed vessel used of God in various areas of ministry from church planter to pastor.

It was my privilege to know him as a fellow minister. It was my privilege to serve in the closing years of his life as his District Superintendent. Most of all, it was a privilege to call him my friend.

I wish just one more time I could lean close and ask him, "Popsey, what's His name?" and hear his reverberating reply: "JESUS!"

I commend his daughters, Nara and Vesta Layne, for their love and loyalty to their parents. They lived out the 5th commandment to "Honor thy father and mother." This book is just one more way of doing just that.

T.F. Tenny

# INTRODUCTION

One of the earliest recollections I have of my father is of his sitting in a cane-bottomed ladder-back chair while bouncing me on his knees and smiling down at me indulgently. I adored him and I wanted to do or say something that would please him; so I looked upwards and with my finger drew a triangle. At each angle of the triangle I said: "There is the father, there is the son, and there is the Holy Ghost." My father just kept smiling and bouncing me on his knees. He knew that my little toddler mind was not ready for a lesson in theology.

When I was ten years old my father gave me a Bible that I still have and treasure greatly. The bible was beautifully bound in black pebbled leather and it had a zipper all the way around. Inside were beautiful pictures in color depicting some of the best known stories in the old and new testaments.

One of the outstanding features of the Bible was a comprehensive concordance located at the back. My father frequently asked me to look up Scriptures for him that he planned to use in a sermon; since I was an avid reader, I eagerly and happily accepted the challenge. Whether he actually needed my help or if this was just his way of getting me interested in reading the Scripture, I'll never know. I do know this: He was a very wise father and I developed a desire to read the Bible. I especially enjoyed the poetic books in the Old Testament.

In September of the year 1943, I suddenly became the only sibling at home. Vesta Layne had just married a young evangelist named Gerald Mangun and Clibborn was a pilot in the United States Air Force. It fell my lot to accompany my parents to Ora, Woden, and Etoile, Texas and other places where they were called to minister.

For the next fourteen years I worked closely with my parents in their ministry and was present when many of the events recorded in this book occurred. My knowledge of the ones that I was not a witness to came from the telling and retelling of the stories to me by my parents.

Many times throughout the passing of years, when I have shared the experiences with others, they have said, "Nara, you should write a book."

For the purpose of readability, I chose to call him "Roy" throughout the book; but he was known as brother Roy, brother Gibson, Reverend Gibson and then "Popsey" Gibson at various stages in his ministry.

Alexander Pope (1688-1744), the English essayist, poet and satirist, once wrote: "the whole is greater than the sum of its parts." And so it was with Royal Denver Gibson. I have attempted to portray the many facets of his life's ministry, passions, and personality, but I have probably fallen way short.

One thing I can say for certain, however, is that none of what is recorded in this book has been exaggerated, over-blown, or enlarged upon in any way. In fact, some of the commentary and telling of events may have been understated or minimized.

I have tried to be objective. And in that, I believe I have succeeded.

Nara Gibson Wenrich
Fall 2011

# THE CONVERSION

*"There was a man sent from God whose Name was John"* (St John 1: 6)

For every generation God has a pre-ordained purpose and He always chooses a man to fulfill that sovereign purpose.

The Pentecostal movement in North America had its beginning in the early twentieth century on Azusa Street in Los Angeles, California. The Movement then spread quickly to other parts of the United States and Canada. By the year 1921, the Movement had reached a small town named Zavalla, which was located in the piney woods of East Texas.

Born October 20, 1890, Royal Denver Gibson was the oldest child of an affluent farmer, cattle rancher, and land holder named Isaiah Argailus Gibson and his wife Narcissus Arizona whose maiden name was Hawkins. Roy, as he was affectionately called, and his wife Eulah Annie lived in a house on the family compound in a small community named Gibsonville. The couple had two small children—a daughter named Nona Ellen and a son named Royal Denver Jr. whom they called R.D. for short.

On a day ordained by God, Roy made a routine trip to the nearby town of Zavalla to buy groceries and necessities for his family. This trip, however, turned out to be anything but routine or ordinary.

As Roy entered the store, his attention was immediately captured by the owner who was talking loudly and excitedly to a few men about a meeting that was being held in a brush arbor on the outskirts of town. Roy joined the group and listened to the owner describe what took place each night at these meetings. It seemed that the preacher would throw powder on them, hypnotize them, and cause them to behave in a strange and erratic manner. The more that Roy heard the more indignant he became. And being a man of character and integrity Roy said impulsively, "Those people ought to be run out of town."

As he rode back to Gibsonville the things Roy had heard at the store kept turning over and over in his mind. Roy decided that he would go to the meeting and "check it all out" for himself.

He said, "I'll keep my mind whirling so they can't hypnotize me."

The first night that Roy attended the meeting, he took a friend with him. Being a little skittish, Roy parked his car as close to the arbor as was possible and he and his friend sat in the car to observe and listen. The car was a T-model Ford that had no top so they were able to see and hear everything that went on.

At first, Roy was amused and laughed uncontrollably. But as the service progressed, he began to get angry and then his anger turned to pity as he decided that the people were sincere but deceived.

On the ride home that evening, Roy decided that he would never go back. However, the next evening Roy could hardly wait to get back to the brush arbor meeting. There was something powerful, but inexplicable, that kept pulling him back night after night. Roy was troubled about his feelings and he went to his uncles who were deacons in the church he grew up in to ask for their advice. Roy's uncles advised him to stay away from "those people" but Roy couldn't stay away.

One day it rained so hard, that it was impossible to hold the meeting under the brush arbor. The preacher went to the city commissioner and obtained his permission to use a community church building for one night. As Roy sat on the back pew completely engrossed in the service, a strange thing happened. Suddenly, the clothes of the small group of singers on the platform changed to glistening white robes and their faces glowed with a radiance that was not common to human faces. To Roy, the group looked like a band of angels and he said with conviction, "I'm lost and I must have what those people have."

As Roy stepped out into the aisle, he heard a voice say, "All these people are looking at you." Roy stopped abruptly but a young man took him by the arm and said, "Brother Roy, let's go pray."

Roy wept bitterly and profusely as he made a full confession of his sins to God but he did not receive the baptism of the Holy Spirit that night. The following night was a repeat of the first night. The third night the minister came to him and said, "Brother Roy, what's wrong?" Roy said, "I don't know—I've done everything you told me to do." The minister then asked Roy if he would like to be baptized in the name of Jesus Christ to have his sins remitted according to Acts 2:38. Without hesitation Roy answered that he wanted to be baptized that very night. Although the hour was late the minister took Roy to the nearest water hole and baptized him in the name of Jesus Christ.

The next day was a complete blur for Roy. He could hardly wait to get back to the service because he knew that something wonderful was going to happen to him. Roy sat on the second pew next to the aisle that night and when the minister gave the invitation to come forward, he took what seemed to him to be one giant step and he was at the altar seeking God with all his heart, soul, mind, and strength. A Methodist preacher was also at the altar that evening but his wife came to him and said, "You had better get away from that man—he might hurt you." A doctor's wife was also at the meeting. As she was standing on a bench observing, she said, "That man is dying and they won't do anything for him."

According to Roy's own words—while he was praying desperately and completely oblivious to anything else that was going on around him, he entered into another realm. When he returned to consciousness, he was standing on his feet, worshipping and praising God and speaking in a language that he did not understand.

After witnessing Roy's powerful "born again" experience, the Methodist preacher returned to the altar and said, "I came here to receive the baptism of the Holy Spirit and I'm going to stay here until I receive it!" He, too, was filled with the Holy Spirit that night.

As they were riding home that evening, Eulah turned to Roy and said, "Let's go back to our old church." Roy looked at her affectionately and said, "Honey, you can go back if that is what you want to do but I can't go back." Roy did not fully understand what had happened to him; but he knew that it was real and that he would never be the same.

The next evening Eulah was also filled with the Holy Spirit and was baptized in the same place where Roy was baptized. From that night forward, Eulah never looked back. Without complaining, Eulah supported Roy in every phase of his ministry. She later said, jokingly, that she would have received the Holy Spirit the same night that Roy did but that he ran everybody away from the altar.

Three years prior to their conversion to the Pentecostal Movement, Roy and Eulah had lost their youngest child—a son, whom they had simply named Ray. Ray was only fourteen months old when he died from a sudden, mysterious illness that lasted only three days. Given Roy and Eulah's penchant for unusual names, one might wonder if the short simple name "Ray" was an unwitting indicator of his short life. At any rate, Ray was a very special child. Not only did he possess an intellect far beyond his age, he was beautiful in every way. Ray was the darling of the family, but he and Roy had a very special bond. The entire family was devastated by Ray's death, but Roy was inconsolable. Even the family pet, a dog named Bringer, left the home and did not return for several days. Roy would walk through the majestic forests of Gibsonville and wonder if he would ever see his darling Ray again. When Roy received the baptism of the Holy Spirit, the grief that had stalked him since Ray's death, vanished. He knew without a doubt that he would, indeed, see his beloved child again.

# CALL TO PREACH

*"Not that I have already attained, or am already perfected, but I press on, that I may lay hold of that for which Christ Jesus has also laid hold of me."*
*(Phil. 3:12 New King James Version)*

It was not yet clear to Roy what he had experienced, but he knew that it was real, it was powerful, and that he would never be the same. Both Roy and Eulah were users of snuff—a fashionable and common practice in those days—and they had tried many times, unsuccessfully, to give up the habit. They would throw away their snuffboxes in the evening and the following morning they would be looking to retrieve them. After their "born again" experience, the craving for the habit left them and never returned.

Roy began a relentless pursuit of God and a deeper understanding of his encounter with Him. Although his rural lifestyle demanded much of his time, Roy would talk to God while he was going about his work throughout the day and he would read his Bible late into the night.

According to Roy, he and God would talk to each other as if they were "face to face."

One day while he and God were having one of their "face to face" talks, God told Roy that He wanted him to preach the Gospel and share his experience with everyone he met. Roy was stunned and began making excuses. He said, "I've never attended a seminary; I have a family to support and I don't have the proper clothes to wear." God answered Roy and said, "If you will listen to me and be obedient, I will supply all your needs, and I will set you on high."

> *Psalm 91:14 "Because He has set His love upon me, therefore will I deliver him; I will set him on high, because he hath known my name."*

Roy began his ministry in a small community called Stumpville. He and another young minister by the name of Bohannan would preach on alternate nights. After the first week, Brother Bohannon became discouraged and left, but Roy continued the revival for two more weeks. At the conclusion of the revival, twenty-one people had been converted and filled with the Holy Spirit in the small sawmill community.

Having completed his first revival, Roy accepted an invitation from the pastor at Doucette, Texas to come and preach a revival for him. The pastor secured a large building located in the center of town for the revival. The building was open on all sides and was not ceiled. When the anointing of the Holy Ghost would rest upon him, Roy would impulsively reach up and grab a rafter. A lady in the audience went all over town, unwittingly, advertising the revival by saying, "Come out and see this preacher chin the rafters." The free advertising was very productive and helped generate more than capacity crowds each night. When the revival ended, the lives of many people had been changed. Some of the people received healing for physical ailments, and all of them witnessed the mighty power of God.

Roy took the family home to Gibsonville and then proceeded on to his next revival, which was in Waterman, Texas. Five people received the baptism of the Holy Spirit the first night.

Roy had just gotten back to his home and family in Gibsonville when he was asked to pastor the church in Zavalla, where he had been converted. After a few necessary plans,

Roy and Eulah, with Nona Ellen and R.D. in tow, moved to Zavalla. This move marked the next phase of Roy's ministry. Because of her winsome ways and God-given talent for music, Eulah was a tremendous asset to Roy's pastoral ministry.

After the birth of their son Ray, the doctor had told Eulah that she could have no more children. However, shortly after moving to Zavalla Eulah gave birth to a fine, healthy boy. The couple named their new son Clibborn Isaiah. The name Isaiah came from Roy's father, Isaiah Argailus Gibson; but the name Clibborn was inspired by a dynamic Pentecostal preacher named Booth Clibborn. Shortly after Roy received his "call" to preach, he attended a conference in Fort Worth, Texas. The evening speaker at the conference was Booth Clibborn and he preached a compelling sermon on the soon coming of Christ. Roy was so affected by the sermon that he believed Christ would return before he could get back to his family.

Four years after Clibborn was born, Eulah gave birth to a girl whom they named Vesta Layne. Eulah said that she was in labor only a very short time and that she was "speaking in tongues" when Vesta Layne was born. Vesta Layne later married a young evangelist, Gerald A. Mangun. The couple evangelized a few years and then settled in Alexandria, Louisiana, where they established a bell-weather church known worldwide for its leadership in growth and evangelism.

Shortly after Vesta Layne was born, God began talking to Roy about going to Huntington, Texas, to preach a revival and build a church. Many of Roy and Eulah's relatives lived in Huntington and when Roy and Eulah embraced and became part of the Pentecostal movement, these same relatives were sharply critical and said that they had disgraced the family. For this reason, Roy and Eulah were reluctant to subject themselves to what they believed would be ridicule and rejection.

Roy continued to procrastinate but God had big plans for Huntington and Roy was the chosen man to fulfill those plans. One day when Roy was making a trip to Gibsonville on foot, a friend happened to be driving by in his car. The friend stopped and offered Roy a ride. Not wanting to inconvenience his friend, Roy offered to stand on the running board of the car rather than sit inside. The plan was that when they got to Roy's destination, the friend would slow down and Roy would jump off. However, things did not go as planned. When the driver slowed down, Roy jumped off but his pant leg somehow got caught on the door of the car. Before the driver could get the automobile stopped, Roy had been dragged several hundred feet. When the car finally came to a stop, Roy disengaged himself from the car; bruised and bleeding, he picked himself up and began to repent and make plans to go to Huntington.

Roy's first priority was to secure the location for the revival. To accomplish this Roy went to his dad's good friend "Uncle" John Renfro, a wealthy Free Methodist cattleman who let Roy use a thirteen-acre parcel of land he owned on the main street. Being a pretty good carpenter himself, Roy engaged the help of a master carpenter, Samuel Thomas. Together they and several helpers soon had the benches, rostrum and pulpit built. To project his strong resonant voice, Roy had a backboard erected behind the pulpit. People who lived four miles away declared that they could hear the preaching while sitting on their front porches.

The revival began and the people of Huntington came to hear the dynamic preaching of the Pentecostal message. The power of the Holy Spirit was present each night and people were delivered from addictions, some were healed of various diseases and afflictions and many were filled with the Holy Spirit.

The elders of the local churches were deeply concerned that many of their members were attending the Pentecostal revival instead of their own churches. The men formed a delegation made up of representatives from each church and went to John Renfro and offered him money to shut the revival down. Mr. Renfro refused to do so and said, "As long as Roy preaches Jesus Christ he can stay on my property." Mr. Renfro would often go to Roy and give him ten dollars, which was a considerable gift at that time.

Undeterred, the group then proceeded to Lufkin and requested an audience with the district attorney, Curtis Finley. At the meeting, the group asked for an injunction against Roy and his on-going revival. Mr. Finley asked them what grounds they were using for such a request. The men replied that Roy did not belong to any organization. Mr. Finley referred to the

Bible and quoted the book of Matthew, chapter eighteen and verse twenty, where it states, *For where two or three are gathered together in my name, there am I in the midst of them.* He went on to say, "That's the best organization that I know of."

The men became angry and said, "You must be fixin' to join up with him." Mr. Finley replied, "No I'm not, but I didn't think you were that kind of men."

So, Roy kept preaching and the people kept coming. At the close of the forty-night revival fifty people had been filled with the Holy Spirit and baptized in the name of Jesus.

R.D. Jr. was a young boy at the time of the revival in Huntington. During family prayer one day, God gave him a vision. He said, "Daddy, I see a pasture full of cattle grazing on the grass." Roy said, "Let's pray again." Then R.D. said, "Those cattle have bonnets and hats on." They prayed again and God showed R.D. that the pasture was the place where the revival was being held and the cattle were the men and women who were in attendance. R.D. said, "Daddy, one man stood up to defy you and come against you but all the people stood with you."

The next evening a prominent man came to the meeting and brought his daughter with him. The daughter went to the altar but her father came to her and forced her to leave. Roy stepped to the podium and said, "I can't keep you from pulling your children out of the altar but you will have to face them when you stand before God on judgment day." The man said heatedly, "Anyone who says I pulled my daughter away from the altar is a liar." He looked menacingly at Roy and stepped forward in a threatening way. At that moment Roy's uncle Marion, who was a formidable looking figure, stepped in front of Roy and faced the man. The man's anger subsided and he went on his way.

When Roy was preparing the site for his revival he designated a special section for his African American friends. The African American group responded even more enthusiastically than the white people. Many of them received the baptism of the Holy Spirit, but at the conclusion of the revival they went back to their former church because segregation of the races was practiced at that time in our history. They did, however, persuade their pastor to invite Roy to preach at their church. Roy accepted and it was a meeting to remember. Many in the congregation became ecstatic and the pastor did not know how to cope. The shaken pastor never invited Roy to preach a second time.

Shortly after the church building and parsonage were completed Roy answered a knock on his door to find one of his African American Converts standing on the porch. She gestured to a large malignant tumor protruding from her forehead. The lady said, "Reverend Gibson, I'm not worthy to come into your house but if you will just stretch forth your hand and pray for me I know I'll be healed." Roy was moved with compassion at her humility and faith and invited her in. Roy anointed her with oil and prayed for her, then sent her on her way. The following day the lady returned rejoicing and praising God and saying loudly, "Reverend Gibson, come see what the Lord has done for me!" The woman's forehead was smooth and there was no evidence of the large, protruding growth that had been there the day before.

# Building Churches

Roy was not content to just settle down and pastor the new flock of converts in Huntington. The fire that had been ignited in his bosom the night he received the Baptism of the Holy Spirit at a brush arbor meeting in Zavalla, Texas, kept driving Roy to keep going. As long as there was a town or community that had not heard the Pentecostal message, Roy could not rest.

After Nara Lee was born, Roy took a tent and went to Nacogdoches, Texas, where he had a big revival. When the revival ended, a young minister, Wesley Mott moved his family to Nacogdoches and built the church. Reverend Mott stayed in Nacogdoches and pastored the church for the remainder of his life.

Roy then set his mind to go to Ora, a small agricultural community not far from Huntington. When the sheriff learned of Roy's plans he went to him and said, "I feel sorry for you because there is a man living there who runs off every preacher who comes to town." Undaunted, Roy went to Ora and received permission to use a communal building which was built for such a purpose.

On the first night of his revival, Roy spotted the man he had been warned about in the audience. At the conclusion of the service Roy went to the man, introduced himself and said, "I've come here to help everyone that I can." The man immediately fell in love with Roy and the next evening he brought a cake and a side of beef to him.

The man made a sincere effort to clean up his life and change his ways. He began by going to the people whom he had defrauded or committed egregious acts against to ask their forgiveness. A few people said they would forgive him but others said they would not. The man became discouraged and reverted back to his former ways. He later went to a public gathering and knocked the wires loose from the spark plugs of a car that was parked at the meeting place. When the irate car owner learned who committed the act, he and his two sons took guns and went looking for the perpetrator. They found him at the communal building where he had gone to take refuge. The victim and his two sons argued over who would shoot the culprit and eventually shot him, ironically, in the place where he had first attempted to reform his life. The man's blood stained the walls of the building and the stains remained there until the building was demolished many years later.

A pioneer and trail blazer, Roy could not rest as long as there was a city, town or community that had not heard the message of Pentecost. Against all odds he had gone to Ora and established a group of believers. Roy then set his sights on Etoile and Woden—two communities that were within a ten to fifteen mile radius of Huntington, Lufkin and Nacogdoches. Both Etoile and Woden were thriving agricultural communities where many good solid families lived. Fueled by an unyielding desire to fulfill the mission that God had placed upon him, Roy went to each of these communities and held revivals. As he had done elsewhere, Roy left a "First Pentecostal Church" in the wake of his revivals.

Since Huntington was his main place of ministry, Roy enlisted Wesley Mott to assist with the church at Woden. Other young ministers whom Roy had mentored assisted him with the churches at Etoile and Ora. During these busy years, Roy still found the time to preach special open-air revivals for other pastors. He went to

Oil City, Louisiana, for a pastor whose name was Echols. At this revival Nara Lee was three years old and Vesta Layne was six years of age. During each night of the revival they sang "special songs" in harmony with their mother, Eulah. The meetings were held under a tent and the crowd was over-flowing each night.

A gentleman who attended the revival wanted to arrange for Eulah and the young girls to sing on the radio. He thought it was quite phenomenal for children that age to sing in perfect harmony. However, the revival ended before this could be arranged.

A few years later, Roy preached another tent revival in Gladewater, Texas for a pastor whose last name was Gary. During a service that lasted quite late, Nara Lee went to sleep on a church bench. When she awakened she saw a five-dollar bill on the ground directly beneath her. At the close of the service Nara Lee took the bill to her father. The crowd, by that time, had dispersed so the next evening Roy announced that his little girl had found the bill and if the owner would come to him after service he would return the bill to him.

After the service a gentleman came to him and said: "Preacher, God told me to put that money in the offering plate and I didn't do it. But you got it anyway."

A short time later Roy was asked to come to Turnertown, Texas for another tent revival. The pastor's last name was Fuller. At the beginning of the revival, Nara Lee and Vesta Layne were playing in a swing under a large oak tree when Nara Lee fell out and knocked her right shoulder out of place. Roy and Eulah put her arm in a sling and it stayed there for three weeks. On the last night of the revival the crowd was such that many were standing at the edge of the tent for lack of seating. The children were asked to sit on the altar benches and Nara Lee was sitting on the end of one. When she turned around to view the audience she fell and knocked her shoulder back into place.

It was at this revival where Corlis Dees was converted to the Pentecostal Movement. He was only a teenager at the time and he later received a "call" from God to preach. He later married Marvelle Mott, a cousin of Roy's, and after evangelizing for a few years the couple pastored the Irvington Pentecostal Church in Houston, Texas.

During his tenure as pastor at the church in Huntington Roy was asked by a man named Modisett to come to Allentown, Texas, to preach a revival. Allentown was a farming community not far from Lufkin and everyone who lived there had the name Allen or Modisett. Two churches were already in existence at Allentown and the pastor of one of the churches was the brother of the gentleman who invited Roy to preach the revival. The gentleman asked his brother for permission to use his church building for the revival, but he refused. Undeterred, Roy and his friend borrowed a tent, gained possession of some benches, and the revival began. Everyone in the area flocked to the Pentecostal tent revival and when the revival ended, more than one hundred people had experienced the infilling of the Holy Spirit. One of the churches had to close its doors but the church that was pastored by the Modisett brother became the home of the "First Pentecostal Church" of Allentown.

For the next several years Roy was busy pastoring the churches he had founded in the wake of his revivals. The church in

Huntington, however, remained the focal point of the ministry. Roy and his family—Eulah, Clibborn, Vesta Layne, and Nara Lee lived in the parsonage, which was located next to the church; and Clibborn, Vesta Layne, and Nara Lee attended school in Huntington.

When the stock market crashed in the year 1929, the entire nation was plunged into the Great Depression. History has recorded the devastating effects the economic meltdown had on the nation. Farmers who owned their land, home, and equipment were able to survive on the bounty of their crops but money was tight and in short supply. Tithes consisted of eggs, produce, and whatever else was grown on the farm. To get money for school supplies and clothes, it was necessary to move the family back to Gibsonville. They moved into one of the houses on the Gibson family compound and raised a crop of cotton, and prayed every night that the price of cotton would remain steady for the next few years. Roy and the family stayed in Gibsonville and commuted on weekends to Huntington and to the other churches when necessary. Many times Roy would hold two to three-week revivals in one of his churches.

When the family left the service late at night, Nara Lee and Vesta Layne would sleep in the back seat of the car until they arrived home in Gibsonville. Then they would be awakened to go in and get in bed only to get up when morning came much too soon. After a breakfast of Eulah's homemade biscuits, butter, and syrup they would catch the bus for school in Zavalla.

It was in the late 1930s that Roy was asked to come to Lufkin and pastor a small church whose former pastor abandoned the church without installing a new pastor. After ardently praying about it, Roy felt that this was what God wanted him to do. Roy moved the family to Lufkin, got them situated in a rented house and began the task of building a strong, spiritual, growing church. The building that the small group was meeting in was in a state of disrepair. However, it was necessary and feasible to continue meeting there for a while. In the meantime, Roy held street meetings every Saturday on the courthouse square. At the conclusion of Roy's short sermon, Nara Lee and Vesta Layne, who played the guitar, sang as the crowd put money in a hat placed on the ground. As a result of these Saturday meetings at the courthouse square, the crowds at the church increased and membership grew.

Roy began making plans to construct a new building for the growing congregation. But first the old unpainted building had to be torn down and every available church member joined in the effort to accomplish this task. Roy gave Nara Lee and Vesta Layne a crowbar each and they helped pry the boards off the studs. Soon the building was completely torn down and the ground was prepared for the new sanctuary. Eulah and a gifted seamstress, Virgie Spurgeon, made sun bonnets and aprons which they went all over town selling. They also went to the merchants in the city and asked for donations to help build the new sanctuary. Most merchants were very generous and there were donations from lumberyards and building supply houses. By this time, Nara Lee had discovered her gift for playing the piano and Roy took a job at the paper mill as a night watchman to earn money to buy a piano for the new building. For the next several years the church continued to prosper and when he was needed Roy would go and minister to the other churches he had founded.

When the family moved to Lufkin, Clibborn stayed with his grandparents at Gibsonville and continued to attend school in Zavalla. When he came of age Clibborn enlisted in the United States Air Force and became a skilled pilot and instructor. In 1943, Vesta Layne met a young, handsome, dynamic evangelist, Gerald Mangun. They became engaged and a few months after she graduated from high school, Vesta Layne and Gerald were married at the First Pentecostal Church in Lufkin.

Roy and Eulah continued pastoring the church in Lufkin for another year, but another change was about to take place in their lives. In the fall of 1944, the pastor of the church in Beaumont, Texas, resigned and left the church assembly before naming his successor. The leadership of the church contacted Roy and asked him if he would come preach for them and consider becoming their next pastor. After much prayer, Roy went to Beaumont and preached for several nights. At the conclusion, the church voted overwhelmingly for Roy to be their new pastor.

The next twenty-six years for Roy and Eulah proved to be some of the most rewarding and productive years of their lives—both personally and in the ministry. The nation was beginning to emerge from the throes of the Great Depression; financial institutions were becoming more stable which eased up credit and businesses, in general, were returning to profitability. Roy set about to restore the good name of the church by paying outstanding bills that were several months in arrears when he became pastor. He went throughout the business community and introduced himself as he extended an invitation to visit the First Pentecostal Church located on Pope Street at the end of Gulf Avenue. Roy soon earned the respect and confidence of Beaumont's business community and elected officials. Once, when a man with no prior criminal record was arrested for breaking into a liquor store, Roy was called to visit him in jail. Roy went to see the individual and talked to him about giving his life to Jesus Christ. When the man was released on a surety bond he brought his family to church and, as a result, the entire family was saved. Because the man turned his life around and became a model citizen, Roy was able to get his record expunged of the offense.

Other factors contributed to the sudden growth of the church membership. Roy purchased airtime on the most listened-to radio station in Beaumont where he hosted a daily fifteen-minute inspirational gospel program. In addition, he brought in evangelists who were true revivalists and other ministries were brought in to advance the education department. As the church membership began to grow in number, it was apparent that a larger, more accommodating building was needed. A building program never intimidated Roy, so he began drawing plans for a new edifice.

The old building, which was quite small, had an exterior of wooden siding. The new structure would be made of brick on the outside and the inside walls of the sanctuary, would be stained hard wood paneling. The floors were hardwood with carpeting down the aisle and on the platform. The prayer room and educational rooms extended behind the sanctuary. The pastor's study was located on one side of the vestibule and a nursery was located on the opposite side.

Before the new building was ready for occupancy, it was necessary to tear down the old building to make room for parking. During the interim period between the demolition of the old building and the completion of the new one, Vesta and Gerald Mangun preached a tent revival north of Beaumont toward the towns of Sour Lake and Lumberton, Texas. The revival lasted eight weeks and several entire families were saved and added to the church. A highway patrolman by the name of Davis was patrolling the area one evening and he stopped out of curiosity to attend the meeting. He was very affected by the service and the following night he brought his whole family to the tent revival. As a result, the entire family was saved and became one of the most faithful and supportive families in the church.

It would be impossible to name the individuals and families who remained faithful and supportive of Roy and Eulah throughout their tenure of service and leadership at the First Pentecostal Church in Beaumont, Texas; but there is no doubt that they will share in the rewards that will be conferred at the Judgment Seat of Christ.

> *"He that receiveth a prophet in the name of a prophet shall receive a prophet's reward." (Matt. 10:4)*

In the fall of 1970, Roy resigned from his church in Beaumont, Texas that he had pastored for twenty-six years. During a business meeting prior to Roy's resignation and under his direction, the church assembly voted for L. Charles (Buck) Treadway to be their new pastor. Roy was eighty years of age.

Soon after his successor was voted in, Roy and Eulah moved from Beaumont, Texas, to Alexandria, Louisiana to be near their two daughters, Vesta Layne and Nara Lee. At the age of eighty Roy's gait was steady and sure, his voice was still vibrant and strong, and his eyes were not dim. Although his church building days were over, Roy's ministry showed no signs of diminishing. Roy carved a niche for himself in the hearts of the people at "The Pentecostals of Alexandria," the church that was pastored by his son-in-law, Gerald Mangun. Roy occupied a prominent place on the platform where children and grown-ups alike would come just to get "Popsey," as he was affectionately called, to lay hands on and pray for them. Roy devoted his time to preaching occasionally during the absence of his son-in-law and he was frequently asked to preach funerals. Roy also performed many weddings at his and Eulah's home for couples that, for various reasons, did not want a church wedding.

When Roy was ninety-two years of age he was interviewed by a reporter for the newspaper, *Alexandria Daily Town Talk*. At the time of the interview, Roy was the oldest active United Pentecostal minister in the United States. When the reporter asked him about his plans to retire, Roy said he had not given much thought to retiring. He said, "Well, if you have something you hate to give it up—something in me just wants to go on."

Roy passed away on the twenty-third day of September in 1989. He was less than one month shy of his ninety-ninth birthday. Although he is no longer here on earth that "Something" in him that "just wanted to go on" is still alive and well. The churches he founded in Angelina and Nacogdoches counties are strong, vibrant, and thriving entities today. There are multiple Pentecostal churches in Lufkin, Beaumont, and Nacogdoches. The Churches located in Huntington, Woden, Ora, Etoile, and Allentown are still proclaiming the Pentecostal message that Roy trail-blazed and heralded many decades ago. At the time of R.D. Jr's death he was a faithful member of the church founded in Huntington. Nona Ellen faithfully attends the church in Lufkin that was pastored and brought to maturity by her father.

Yes Roy, "something in you" is still going on.

*Roy and Eulah shortly after their wedding*
*in Huntington, Texas*

*In front of the new church building
in Beaumont, Texas*

*With son-in-law G.A. Mangun at
50th wedding anniversary*

*Royal Denver Gibson—*
*revival and church building era*

*R.D. Gibson with grandson*
*Anthony Mangun*

*Roy and Eulah—"Old Fashioned Sunday"*
*in Jackson, MS*

*Royal D. Gibson giving invocation in Alexandria, LA*

*Reverend Gibson preaching at the age of 90 in Alexandria, LA*

*Reverend Gibson at age 95*
*officiating at a wedding*

*Momsey Gibson celebrating 100 years of age with her children, from left clockwise: Nona, Nara Lee. R.D. Jr., Clibborn and Vesta Mangun*

# HEALING THE SICK AND RAISING THE DEAD

A Comparison can be made between the conversion of Saul of Tarsus and Roy Gibson of Gibsonville, Texas. The ninth chapter of the book of Acts relates how Saul was on his way to Damascus with letters from the high priests in his possession to apprehend all—whether men or women—who were followers of Jesus Christ and bring them bound to Jerusalem.

However, as Saul and his entourage were enroute to Damascus for that purpose and intent, he had a supernatural encounter with God. Saul saw a bright light and heard a voice from heaven calling his name. Saul was blinded and fell from his horse to the ground. Then he and God had a conversation. In their "face to face" talk God gave Saul explicit instructions on where to go and what to do to be saved. Paul obeyed and after three days of fasting and praying he was filled with the Holy Ghost, the "scales" fell from his eyes and his eyesight was restored and he was baptized. The entire story of Paul's conversion is recorded in the ninth chapter of the book of Acts in the New Testament.

When Roy heard about the "fanatics" and their brush arbor meeting, his intent was to "run them out of town." But God intercepted Roy's plan with a plan of his own. When God gave him the heavenly vision that fateful night in Zavalla, Texas, Roy knew what he must do to be saved. And God knew that this strong-willed man with an indomitable spirit would need an extraordinary experience to enable and empower him to accomplish the formidable work that he was destined to do for the Kingdom of God.

After his powerful encounter with God the night he was filled with the Holy Ghost, Roy began to read his Bible passionately and search its Scriptures. He believed it said what it meant and meant what it said. When he read Mark 16:17, 18 Roy accepted it unequivocally and began to preach and practice it.

> [17] *"And these signs shall follow them that believe. In my name shall they cast out devils; they shall speak with new tongues"* [18] *"They shall lay hands on the sick and they shall recover."*

At the beginning of each revival, Roy would announce that each Friday night would be devoted to praying for the sick. He would say, "It doesn't matter what is wrong with you or how long you've been ill or infirm—I will anoint you with oil, pray for you and God will heal you." Then he would quote James 5:15.

> *"And the prayer of faith will save the sick and the Lord will raise him up."*

Eulah said she dreaded to hear this announcement because almost without exception one of the children would become very ill when Roy set aside a special healing service.

On one such occasion Clibborn was beset by a dangerously high fever during the night. There was no apparent reason for the extremely elevated temperature and Roy and Eulah suspected that it was an assault from Satan. The couple rebuked the devil and ordered him to leave the house. Clibborn's fever subsided immediately and the couple said that they saw the evil one leave by way of the window. When asked what he looked like, they each concurred that he was dressed in sooty black clothes and wore a soot-covered black hat. He looked like a boiler room worker to them.

In Huntington, a lady named Rosie Snowden came to the church for the first time to attend a New Year's Eve service. Rosie was an accomplished seamstress but she had a congenital deformity that affected one of her feet and caused her to walk with a limp. She heard that when Roy prayed for the sick and afflicted, they recovered. Rosie came forward for prayer and Roy perceived that she had the faith to be healed. He anointed her with oil and prayed for her in the Name of Jesus. God healed her life-long infirmity and filled her with His Holy Spirit.

Rosie's husband, strangely enough, was angry that she had attended the Pentecostal Church and threatened to do bodily harm to Roy. Shortly thereafter as Mr. Snowden was crossing the road in front of his home, a car hit him and broke both of his legs. He then called Roy to come and pray for him.

While pastoring the church in Huntington Roy was summoned late at night to the home of one of his church members. The young son of this family had contracted the highly contagious disease of diphtheria. The disease is characterized by a false membrane that forms in the air passages of the lungs and severely constricts breathing. The disease is also accompanied by a high fever and extreme weakness. In that era the medical establishment had no cure or remedy and diphtheria was usually fatal.

The man who drove Roy to the home of the sick child parked his car on the side of the road in front of the house. Roy said that before he exited the car he could hear the boy struggling to breathe. When Roy entered the room where the child lay he anointed him with oil and prayed but he said he could tell that his prayer went no further than the ceiling. Roy went to the back porch of the home and looked up at the beautiful moonlit, star-studded sky. While he was standing there in awe and wonder of God's creation God spoke to him and said, *"Go back and pray for the child one more time."* Roy went back to the room, laid his hand on the child and prayed again. Immediately the child's breathing became normal, his fever subsided and he sat up in bed and asked for food.

While Roy was preaching in Woden, Texas, a man who had an advanced case of tuberculosis came to the service for prayer. His doctor had given him no hope for recovery because x-rays showed that his lungs were so scarred and ravaged by the disease they were barely functioning. The man whose last name was Thrailkill was desperate for help because he had a wife and young children to support. After Roy anointed him with oil and prayed the prayer of faith, Mr. Thrailkill went back to his doctor and requested a second X-ray. To the amazement of his doctor, the X-ray showed that his lungs were perfectly healthy and there was no evidence of the pernicious disease that had been there earlier.

At eight years of age, Nara Lee became very ill with bronchial pneumonia. Her fever soared to a dangerous level and she soon lapsed into a coma. In spite of Roy's faith in the healing power of God he was overcome by fear and he sent for brother Wesley Mott to come and pray for her. Roy and Wesley were colleagues in the ministry and they shared a mutual trust and respect for each other.

Brother Mott walked into the child's bedroom where family members, including her paternal grandmother, had gathered to keep vigil. After anointing her with oil, brother Mott prayed a fervent faith-filled prayer. Nara Lee opened her eyes, her fever left and she was able to return to school in a couple of days.

> *"And the prayer of faith shall save the sick and the Lord shall raise him up."* *(James 5:15)*

When Nona and R.D. Jr. were young children, the family milk cow became disabled. When the cow would lie down, she would be unable to get back up. In order to milk the cow, the entire family would have to go with their combined strength and physically help the cow to stand on her feet. One morning, before they went out to perform this chore, R.D. said, "Daddy, why don't we just pray and ask God to heal the cow?" The four of them knelt down and began praying for God to heal the cow and restore her to normal. While they were praying Nona looked out the window and said excitedly, "Daddy! Daddy! The cow is getting up!" God healed the cow and they never had to help her get up again.

At five years of age, Clibborn jumped over a fence to shoo a chicken out of the family garden. Unfortunately, he landed on a rusty rake and the prongs of the rake went completely through his foot. Eulah heard the child screaming and ran quickly to check on him. When she saw the severity of the injury her heart almost stopped beating. Mustering every ounce of strength that she had, she pulled the child off the rake and took him inside. Soon tetanus—an acute infectious disease, characterized by rigid spasmodic contractions of the neck and jaw—set in. The incident occurred at mid-morning and Roy and Eulah stayed by his bedside all day, praying. Eulah said that at late afternoon, the room was suddenly filled with the presence of God. The muscles of Clibborn's jaw and neck relaxed, his fever left him and God filled him with His Holy Spirit.

Shortly after Vesta and Gerald were married, they were invited to preach a tent revival at a Pentecostal church in Cleveland, Texas. Since Lufkin was only a two-hour drive away, Roy and Eulah decided to make the trip and be with them in the service. They arrived a bit early and discovered that Vesta had an acute case of tonsillitis. Her tonsils were badly swollen and inflamed and she was running a high fever. When her father anointed her with oil and prayed for her, God performed a tonsillectomy and she spit the diseased tonsils out. Vesta was able to sing and play her accordion in the service that night.

Roy and Eulah had been pastoring the church in Beaumont for approximately one year when Roy answered a knock on his front door. The gentleman standing there introduced himself as Al Debes and asked, "Are you brother Gibson?" Roy confirmed that he was and the man continued by saying, "They tell me that when you pray for the sick they are healed."

Roy invited Al into his home and as the story unfolded Roy learned that Mr. Debes was a recent convert from the Greek Orthodox Church to the Pentecostal faith and that he was a member of the Pentecostal church located in Vidor, Texas. Vidor is just across the Neches River from Beaumont. Al told Roy that a sliver of steel had accidentally pierced his eyeball and damaged the pupil. His ophthalmologist told him that he would lose sight in the affected eye. Roy said, "Nothing is impossible with God. He can heal your eye!" After anointing

Al with oil, Roy prayed and asked God to heal his eye completely. A second visit to the doctor confirmed that Al's eye had completely recovered from the injury and his vision was 20/20.

After God healed his eye, Al was a frequent visitor to the Gibson home. In his earlier years Al had been a prizefighter but he was now a wholesale distributor of fresh produce. Al would often bring fresh vegetables and fruit on his visits to the home and Roy would mentor him in his faith.

Al learned about a young mother whose toddler had fallen victim to the dreaded disease of diphtheria. The child had been hospitalized and was in isolation at the *Hotel Dieu* hospital in Beaumont. The mother was a member of the large church downtown and even though Roy did not know her he agreed to visit her and pray for the child.

When Roy ascended the stairs and reached the third floor he saw the woman's pastor talking to her and overheard him say, "If there's anything I can do let me know." Roy waited discreetly for the Reverend to leave and then he knocked on the child's door. When the mother opened the door Roy introduced himself and said, "I've come to pray for your child to be healed."

The mother began to weep and opened the door for Roy to come inside. He then asked her, "Do you believe that God can heal your baby?" She fell to her knees and said with conviction, "Oh Yes, I do!" Roy anointed the child with oil and said, "In the Name of that Holy child, Jesus, heal this baby." He turned to the mother and said, "Your child is healed." From that very moment the child began to improve and the following day his pediatrician pronounced him well and ordered his release from the hospital.

At another time, Al drove brother Gibson to the home of a woman who had congestive heart failure and was near death. The lady's doctor had released her from the hospital because she had not responded to any treatment and there was nothing else he could do. During the drive to the woman's house God brought the story of Jesus' raising Lazarus from the dead to Roy's mind. He knew then that God was going to heal her.

When they arrived at the lady's home they went to her bedroom and saw that she was unresponsive and barely breathing. Some of her relatives were in the room and Roy said to them, "If there is anyone in this room who does not believe that God is going to heal this woman, I ask that you please leave the room." With the exception of one woman, everyone left the room. The remaining lady said to Roy, "I dip snuff—would that hinder?" Roy told her it might be better if she left also.

When Roy anointed her with oil and began praying the woman jumped up in bed and said, "The Lord just gave me a new heart!" Several years later she was seen at a fellowship meeting still praising and worshipping God.

### A Testimony Given By Carrie Dickerson, Beaumont, Texas

One Wednesday night at a regular church service I was sitting by sister Barbee when suddenly her head dropped and she fell forward. She had stopped breathing and she had no pulse or heartbeat. Brother Gibson was at the pulpit and when he saw the commotion, he knew instinctively that something was wrong. He grabbed his little bottle of oil, stepped down from the pulpit and started walking toward us. I said, "It's no use, brother Gibson, she's dead." Brother Gibson said, "Maybe not." He anointed her with oil and prayed; she gave a loud gasp and began breathing again. All who were present fell to their knees and began to worship God. Sister Barbee lived quite a few years after that incident and eventually died of cancer.

Sister Carroll, who pastored the Pentecostal church in High Island, Texas during the time that Roy pastored in Beaumont, became very ill with a debilitating sickness that the doctors were unable to diagnose; therefore they could not prescribe a treatment. Her health continued to decline until she was bedridden. The doctors told her that if her condition did not improve soon she would die.

Roy heard about Sister Carroll's illness and he felt an urgency to go pray for her. When he arrived at her home and walked into her bedroom he felt an anointing of power and boldness come upon him. He said to her, "Sister Carroll, the doctors have told you that you are going to die, but I've come here to tell you that you are not going to die—you are going to live!" Roy anointed her with oil then he rebuked death and commanded that her health be restored. He told her to get up and eat because she was healed.

Sister Carroll was able to pastor her church for many more years before she retired and moved to Alexandria, Louisiana to live out the remaining years of her life.

A gentleman in Beaumont who had been blind since birth was brought to Roy for prayer that his vision would be restored. Roy talked to him about repentance and baptism. The man repented of his sins and was baptized. When Roy anointed him with oil and prayed God restored the man's sight.

The gentleman remained faithful to God and the church for a short while; but then he reverted back to his former life and said that he only went to church to get his eyes opened. Shortly thereafter, the man went blind again.

Not only were there miracles of divine healing throughout Roy's ministry, there were also miracles of divine providence.

Nara Lee was born in 1929—the year of the historic stock market crash that caused the Great Depression. Money was scarce and times were hard. A lady, Danny Sims, came to stay in the home and help care for the family while Eulah was recuperating from childbirth.

Many years later after Roy and Eulah were retired and living in Alexandria, Louisiana, Danny located them and traveled from Monroe, Louisiana to visit. Nara Lee happened to be present at the time of Danny's visit and although she had heard her mother tell the story many times, she listened with fascination as Danny told it again in her own words.

WHEN I ARRIVED AT THE HOME OF BROTHER AND SISTER GIBSON IN HUNTINGTON I LOOKED IN THE CUPBOARD AND THERE WAS HARDLY ANY FOOD. SISTER EULAH LOOKED AT BROTHER ROY AND SAID IN A SCOLDING MANNER, "ROY, WHAT ARE WE GOING TO FEED DANNY?" BROTHER ROY LOOKED AT SISTER EULAH AND SAID, "IT'LL BE ALRIGHT HONEY." WITH THAT SAID BROTHER ROY DISAPPEARED. SOON AFTER HE DISAPPEARED, A LONG, SHINY, BLACK SEDAN PULLED UP TO THE HOME AND DELIVERED ENOUGH GROCERIES TO FEED THE FAMILY FOR A MONTH.

Later it was learned that Roy had slipped away to pray. His favorite place of prayer was a secluded oak grove, not far from the parsonage. The mysterious benefactor and his long, black car were never seen again.

During his twenty-six years of pastoring the church in Beaumont, Roy won many people, many souls, to Jesus Christ. His appeal spanned the age chasm from the young to the elderly. Many young couples were among his converts and one particular couple was Dewey and Helen Ellis. Dewey was a master roofer whose expertise was invaluable to Roy's building projects. But beyond that, Dewey and Helen were devoted to their pastor and believed strongly in him because their lives were so changed when he led them to Christ.

When Roy passed away September 23, 1989, Helen drove from Beaumont, Texas to Alexandria, Louisiana to attend his funeral. After the service, Helen went next door to the WHITE STEEPLE BOOKSTORE and requested every tape, compact disc or anything else they had concerning her former pastor. Tanya Lumpkin Nordstrom was assisting Helen and she listened while Helen related this story:

Our daughter overdosed on drugs when she was a teenager. She was hospitalized and was being kept alive on life support. Her doctor came to me in the waiting room and said they were getting ready to remove the life support from my daughter because she was not responding to the treatment. He went on to say there were no brain waves and no sign of life in her body. I immediately said, "Not until I call my pastor!" I called brother Gibson and he came right away to the hospital. He went to our daughter, anointed her with oil and while he was praying our daughter gave a huge gasp, opened her eyes and began breathing! We were able to take our daughter that same day.

A dear lady came to Nara Lee during the wake that was held for brother Gibson and told her this story:

"I HAD A GROWTH ON MY EYELID THAT THE DOCTOR WOULD NOT REMOVE BECAUSE THE PROCEDURE WAS TOO RISKY. I WENT TO POPSEY GIBSON ONE WEDNESDAY NIGHT AFTER PRAYER MEETING AND ASKED HIM TO PRAY THAT GOD WOULD REMOVE THE GROWTH. POPSEY PRAYED FOR MY EYE AND THE NEXT

MORNING WHILE I WAS WASHING MY
FACE, THE GROWTH CAME OFF AND
ONTO MY WASHCLOTH."
LULA MAE JACKSON
ALEXANDRIA, LA

Shortly after Roy received the gift of the
Holy Ghost on the night of August 4, 1921,
God gave him a revelation of the power that is
embodied in the name of Jesus. The third chapter
of the book of Acts in the New Testament tells
the story of the first apostolic miracle that was
performed after the day of Pentecost.

Peter and John were on their way to the
temple to pray when a lame man, who sat daily
by the Gate Beautiful, asked alms of them.
Peter said, "Look on us! Silver and gold I do
not have but what I do have I give you: In the
name of Jesus Christ of Nazareth, rise up and
walk." And the lame man not only stood and
walked—he went into the temple leaping and
praising God.

After a brief sermon, Peter tells the awe-
struck crowd that it was not his and John's
power that healed the lame man—it was the

name of Jesus—through faith in His name that made the man whole. (Paraphrased; Acts 3:16)

Roy never exploited the gift that God conferred upon him at the beginning of his ministry; nor did he ever use it for personal gain. There was never any effort to sensationalize the miracles and gifts of healing that occurred throughout his ministry. Roy knew that power with God came through unwavering faith in His Word and in the power of the name of Jesus.

A lady in Alexandria, a prayer warrior, had a vision just weeks before Roy passed away in which there was a great throng of people waiting to welcome him to his Eternal home. The throng consisted of all the ones whose lives were changed by his ministry.

The account of miracles contained in this chapter is only a microcosm, a snapshot, of the wonderful acts that God performed through a man whose life was changed when he came "face to face" with God and surrendered to His will. Only Eternity will reveal the full impact that Roy had on his sphere of influence for the Kingdom of God.

*Popsey, you have inscribed your name on the walls of Eternity and left your footprints on the sands of this earth. The generations that follow you will know that Royal Denver Gibson has been here.*

# ROYAL DENVER, THE MAN

Roy was the first of ten children born to Narcissus Arizona Hawkins and Isaiah Argailus Gibson. Since he was the oldest child, Roy assumed responsibility at an early age, not only because it was expected of him, it was also his nature.

The family estate consisted of approximately 600 acres. Sixty acres were set aside for the cultivation of various kinds of crops and part of the land was home to a dense forest of magnificent, virgin pine, and hardwood trees. The remainder of the land was pasture for the cattle, horses, and other livestock to graze upon.

In addition to the large family home, two other houses fronted Gibson Lane. At any given time, members of the Gibson family occupied one or both of the houses.

Roy's mother Narrie, as she was affectionately called, was a pious, God-fearing woman who took her children to church regularly. Roy had an affinity for preachers and was always delighted to be in their company. Both Narrie and Gail were exemplary parents and gave their children a proper upbringing. The daughters were educated to be schoolteachers, one of the few professions that accepted women, and the sons were schooled in business and agriculture.

When Roy reached the age of twenty-one, he accompanied his family to a "cemetery working" which usually took place once each year. The purpose of the event was to clean the graves of leaves and debris and beautify the grounds. However, it soon evolved into a social gathering where each family would bring food and then it would be combined and shared by all. The men talked about politics and the price of corn, cotton, and cattle. The women's conversation centered around child-rearing, cooking, and domestic issues.

It was at one of these gatherings where Roy met Eulah Annie Hudiburgh and he was immediately attracted to her. Although she was only fifteen years of age a courtship ensued and on November 29, 1911 the couple became man and wife.

Roy and Eulah moved into one of the houses that fronted Gibson Lane on the Gibson estate; and they began a journey that took many twists and turns during its span of seventy-eight years.

For the next ten years Roy continued to oversee the affairs of the Gibson estate. During this time, three children were born to the couple: Nona Ellen, R.D. Jr., and Ray. The setting and environment in which Roy was reared molded his character, set his moral compass and influenced his perspective on life. Roy was determined to give his family every advantage that was available in the culture of his day. But as the eighteenth-century Scottish poet Robert Burns (1759-1796) wrote in his poem "Ode To A Mouse" —"the best laid plans of mice and men often go awry." So it was with Royal Denver Gibson. The night he visited a Pentecostal brush arbor meeting in Zavalla, Texas changed his plans and the course of his life forever.

Roy was thirty-one years of age when he received the "call" from God to preach and for the next sixty-eight years he fulfilled that call by preaching in every place where a door was opened to him. From Ora, Etoile, Woden, and Nacogdoches to Zavalla, Huntington, Lufkin, Beaumont and all places in between, Roy preached the Gospel of Jesus Christ without fear of or favor to anyone. He never missed an opportunity to preach the Gospel for lack of transportation. He once walked five miles to an engagement and then after preaching he walked the five miles again back home. His pay for the evening was a fresh ham, which he carried on his shoulder.

The cars that Roy drove during the first half of his ministry were used cars that were sometimes temperamental and unreliable. Yet, despite hardships, he persevered in his relentless effort to further the Kingdom of God. It was not until the latter part of his ministry that he was able to drive a new car.

The values that were instilled in the young Royal Denver while he was growing up remained with him throughout his lifetime. Roy chose to live in the plain simple parsonage that he and Eulah moved into when he accepted the role of pastor at the church in Beaumont. Always putting the Kingdom of God first, Roy delayed building a home for himself until he built the new, more spacious building for his expanding congregation.

Roy's skills as a carpenter enabled him to minimize the construction costs of the new church building. The number of bricks he ordered for the exterior of the new building was so exact that there was only one brick left over when the brick masons completed the job.

After his congregation settled into the new building Roy began to draw plans for a home for himself. He purchased a lot located at 2993 Grand Avenue, which was in a non-elitist middle-class neighborhood, and proceeded to build a modest wooden framed house. After living in this home for approximately ten years, Roy purchased a lot in a slightly better neighborhood and built a three-bedroom brick veneer home where they lived until he retired in 1970. Shortly after retirement, Roy sold the home, and he and Eulah moved to Alexandria, Louisiana where they lived out the remainder of their years.

## As A Husband

From the time that Roy pledged his love to Eulah he never faltered in his effort to provide for her in every way. Once when struggling to get through hard times, Roy was offered a job by the railroad to be a conductor on one of their trains. The salary offered was $400 per month, a pittance by today's standards, but a very handsome salary at that time. Roy was tempted to accept the offer, which would necessitate his leaving the ministry; but God let him know that there would be serious consequences if he forsook his calling. Roy repented to God and never looked back again.

While they were still living in Gibsonville, Roy attempted more than once to teach Eulah to drive. Each time, after driving about a mile, Eulah would get a severe headache. She eventually told Roy that she had no desire to learn to drive and from that time on he drove Eulah wherever she needed to go.

When they married, Roy gave Eulah a modest little wedding band that had gotten lost somewhere along the way. After they moved to Beaumont, Roy took Eulah shopping at one of her favorite dress shops in downtown Beaumont. While she was shopping, Roy disappeared for a while. When he returned, Eulah had finished her shopping and he very excitedly said to her, "Honey, come with me—there's something I want you to see." They walked down the street to a jewelry store where the manager brought out several wedding bands that Roy had asked him to set aside. Eulah chose a plain yellow gold band and Roy slipped it on her finger.

The love that bound them together had been tested by adversity, blessings, triumph, and tragedy. Through it all their love emerged stronger, tougher, and more mature. At the time of Roy's death the couple had celebrated seventy-eight years of marriage. There was never a hint or whisper of infidelity or impropriety on the part of either of them.

## AS A FATHER

As a parent, Roy always desired to provide every possible advantage to his children that would enable them to advance spiritually as well as materially. Coming from a family of educators, Roy knew the importance of education. He believed that a good education plus a firm faith in God and a right sense of work ethics would insure the success of anyone in this life.

Because their lives were somewhat austere, at times, Roy wanted the children to experience "fun times" for balance. When the family schedule permitted, he and Eulah took them to a pristine creek to swim. Eulah was apprehensive about these outings because she was afraid of water but she always made sure that treats—like teacakes or biscuits and ham—were taken along.

On nights when there was no church service to attend, Roy would sometimes go to the kitchen and make a batch of candy out of cane syrup and freshly shelled raw peanuts. The concoction was delicious and Clibborn, Vesta Layne, and Nara Lee looked forward to these treats.

On Christmas morning, the children knew that there would always be a gift for them under the freshly cut Christmas tree which was trimmed with home-made decorations. One Christmas Roy made a small table and two small chairs for the girls. In each chair was a doll and a dainty little tea set graced the table. Nara Lee and Vesta Layne were ecstatic.

For Clibborn there would be a bicycle; perhaps a harmonica—which he played very well—or maybe something else he had wished for.

The legacy that Roy left his children was a lifetime of prayers. He prayed with his children each morning before they left for school. He prayed for God to put a hedge of protection around them, both physically and mentally while they were away. Although the prayers changed in nature and content as his children matured, Roy prayed for each child and each grandchild daily until he lapsed into a coma three days before his death. After his health deteriorated, he would roll his wheelchair to the kitchen window and as he looked out at the dark starry night, he would call each child by name and tell God where he or she lived. These prayers are as viable and effectual today as they were then. According to the book of Revelation, chapter five and verse eight, the prayers are stored in heaven and kept in golden vials.

## AS A PASTOR

From the time that Roy assumed his role as a pastor—beginning with the church he founded in Huntington—he embraced it and fulfilled his duties with consummate passion and dedication. The hour was never too late or too early for Roy to go to the aid of a family or individual who was sick, dying or otherwise in need of help. Roy made himself available to the town officials and gained their favor; consequently, they called upon him to preach funerals and assist those who were in need of spiritual assistance but had no church affiliation. By succoring these families and individuals, Roy led many people to Christ.

Roy had great empathy for widows with children and families who were struggling to make ends meet. Many times when they paid their tithes to him he would thank them and then he would give the money back to them saying, "You've been obedient by paying your tithes to the church and now I'm returning them as my gift to you. God bless you."

For Roy to live was Christ. He never passed up an opportunity to witness to anyone about what Jesus Christ had done in his life. While pastoring the church in Lufkin, he frequented a men's store whose owner/manager was Jewish.

While he was looking at merchandise, Roy witnessed to the owner about his personal experience and how it had changed his life. The gentleman said, facetiously, that he believed the only way a gentile could be saved would be to carry a Jew on his back to Jerusalem. Roy replied, "Well, you just hop on my back and we'll get going!" The owner became very fond of Roy and often gave him deep discounts on his purchases.

Roy's reputation for honesty and good character gained him the respect of the city and county leaders and elected officials. In early December of the year 1941, Roy took his two young daughters, Nara Lee and Vesta Layne to downtown Lufkin for some light shopping. At noon they stopped in at a popular café for the rare treat of a hamburger.

While they were enjoying their meal, the county judge, Butler Ralston, stopped by their table to chat briefly with Roy. As he turned to leave he gave each of the young girls a shiny new half-dollar and wished them a Merry Christmas. The gift was enough to buy each of them a large sack of fruit and mixed nuts.

## ROY'S PRAYER LIFE

Prayer was the fuel that generated the favor and power of God in Roy's life. He prayed when life was going well; he prayed when it seemed that circumstances were stacked against him. When problems and difficulties surrounded him, Roy forged straight ahead saying, *"God is a very present help in trouble"* (Ps. 46:1).

After he retired and moved to Alexandria, Louisiana, Roy made a road trip to Beaumont alone. During the drive and before he reached the state line of Texas a torrential rain quickly flooded the road. The water soon rose past the wheels of the car and the engine died. Roy made several futile attempts to re-start the car. Suddenly he cried out, "Jesus! Get me out of here!" The car started and Roy went on his way. When Roy prayed—things happened!

From the night of August 4, 1921 when Roy had a life-changing encounter with God he began a prayer-life that only intensified with each passing year. He taught the importance of prayer to his family—not only by example—but also by providing time each day for family prayer.

He taught his church members the importance and value of a consistant prayer life. Roy's own life exemplified the power of prayer. Many times at the beginning of a service Roy would invite everyone who was present to gather around the altar for corporate prayer.

The service that followed was filled with the power of God and wonderful things happened.

A member of Roy's church in Beaumont, who was a personal convert of his, committed to mowing and caring for the church lawn. Brother Goss said that on most occasions Brother Gibson would meet him and ask if he had taken time to pray that day. If he had not, his pastor would say, "Come inside and let's pray." Brother Goss said these times of prayer with his pastor kept him faithful to God and kept him from falling into sin.

Roy never wrote down his sermons or even used an outline. During prayer, God gave him the topic for his sermon and the Scriptures he should use. Roy jotted down the Scriptures and then preached as the anointing of the Holy Ghost flowed through him.

At a minister's conference Roy preached a sermon entitled, "The Thing that is hidden from you." The Scripture that inspired this sermon was 2 Corinthians 4:3.

> *"But if our gospel be hid it is hid to them that are lost."*

Because the sermon was preached with such fervor and anointing, many of the ministers asked if they could borrow his notes. Unfortunately, for them, Roy had no notes. One young minister, who was not at the conference, heard others talking about it and came by Roy's home and requested to see his notes on the sermon.

A TESTIMONY BY HORACE AND ELIZABETH SAVANT, BEAUMONT, TEXAS

"HORRACE AND I USED TO CLEAN THE OLD CHURCH IN BEAUMONT. WE NOTICED TWO WORN SPOTS IN THE CARPET ON THE PLATFORM IN FRONT OF BROTHER GIBSON'S CHAIR. WE COULD NEVER FIGURE OUT WHY THEY WERE WORN MORE THAN THE REST OF THE CARPET. ONE DAY HORACE WENT BY THE CHURCH TO TALK WITH BROTHER GIBSON AND HE DISCOVERED THE ANSWER TO THE PUZZLEMENT. THIS WAS BROTHER GIBSON'S PRAYER SPOT. HIS CONSISTENT KNEELING LITERALLY WORE HOLES IN THE CARPET. WE TREASURE THE HERITAGE, WHICH HE LEFT TO HIS CONVERTS AS WELL AS HIS FAMILY: A HERITAGE OF STRENGTH

IN HIS CONDUCT, HIS PRAYERS, AND HIS MESSAGE.

WE FEEL SO THANKFUL AND PRIVILEGED TO HEAR THE ECHOES IN OUR SOULS OF HIS MIGHTY PRAYERS AND THE SCRIPTURES, WHICH FLOWED FROM HIM AS HE PREACHED.

I'VE SEEN HIM DOWNTOWN BEAUMONT, STOPPED AT A TRAFFIC LIGHT AND SPEAKING IN TONGUES WHILE IN PRAYER, MORE THAN ONCE.

WHEN ANYONE IN OUR FAMILY WAS SICK, IT NEVER OCCURRED TO US TO CALL A DOCTOR. WHATEVER THE MALADY—BE IT MEASLES OR 'FLU', WE CALLED BROTHER GIBSON FOR PRAYER. I DO NOT REMEMBER ONE TIME WHEN WE FAILED TO RECEIVE OUR HEALING.

ONE TIME AT WEDNESDAY MORNING PRAYER MEETING IN THE OLD CHURCH, OUR DAUGHTER, A TODDLER, STEPPED BAREFOOT ON THE GRATE OF THE FLOOR FURNACE, WHICH WAS VERY HOT. IT BURNED A GRID PATTERN INTO THE BOTTOM OF HER TINY FOOT. OF COURSE, BROTHER GIBSON ANOINTED

HER WITH OIL AND PRAYED FOR HER. YOU COULD LITERALLY SEE THE ANGRY, RED PATTERN BEGIN TO FADE. BY THE AFTERNOON, THE BURN HAD COMPLETELY DISAPPEARED."

A TESTIMONY BY MELBA AND DUTCH DUPREE IN BEAUMONT, TEXAS

"ONE DAY BROTHER GIBSON CAME TO OUR HOME TO INVITE US TO CHURCH. WE WERE ON THE PATIO SHELLING PEAS AND BROTHER GIBSON PULLED UP A CHAIR AND BEGAN TO SHELL PEAS WITH US. AS HE SHELLED PEAS, HE TALKED ABOUT THE LORD AND HIS GREATNESS. BY THE TIME HE LEFT, WE KNEW THAT WE WOULD BE GOING TO THE CHURCH WHERE HE PREACHED. THE FOLLOWING WEEKEND WE ATTENDED HIS CHURCH AND WERE FILLED WITH THE HOLY SPIRIT AND WERE BAPTIZED."

Roy's prayers were not merely for his family, church and city, his prayers were all-encompassing for the nation and the entire world. When he prayed for specific individuals and situations, he always concluded the prayer with this inclusive petition: "And I pray for those—the world over—whom I should pray for that you would sanctify them and keep them in your Holy care."

During World War II, Germany was our enemy and Russia, the Soviet Union, was our ally. Germany was advancing farther into the Soviet Union's territory every day and it seemed that their army was unstoppable. Roy was very troubled because he knew that Germany—Hitler— would be greatly enriched by the conquest and acquisition of the Soviet Union.

One night while Roy was praying earnestly and fervently for the Russians, God gave him a vision. In the vision he saw a fat, black Holstein bull engaged in a fierce battle with a skinny red longhorn steer. Their horns were locked and the black bull, which represented Germany, had a clear advantage and was pushing the skinny red steer back. All of a sudden the skinny red steer, which represented Russia, got the upper hand and began pushing the black bull back. The headlines of the Beaumont Enterprise on the following day read "RUSSIAN ARMY ROUTS THE GERMANS IN A DECISIVE VISTORY!"

In January of the year 1987, Anthony Mangun, Roy's grandson and the son of Vesta and Gerald Mangun, dedicated the new, magnificent church building that he and his wife, Mickey, built when they moved from Plano, Texas to be senior pastors to the Pentecostals of Alexandria. Anthony asked his grandfather, Roy "Popsy" Gibson, to pray the dedicatory prayer. "Popsy" was ninety-six years of age at the time and although his voice was not as strong as it once had been, it still resonated with power, authority, and anointing.

### *Prayer of Dedication*

*Thank you, Jesus!*

*Lord, Thou has been our dwelling place in all generations. Before the mountains were brought forth, or ever Thou hadst formed the world and everything therein, from everlasting to everlasting, Thou art God. Thou turnest man to destruction; and sayest, Return, ye children of men.*

*A thousand years in thy sight are as yesterday when it is passed and gone and like a watch in the night. Lord, we come forth like a flower of the field. We*

93

*continue, Lord a little while. When the evening comes, we are cut down.*

*We thank You Lord for this privilege that we have come to the evening time. And here we are in a church, Lord, dedicated to You and we pray You, dear Lord, that You would be with us and that You would guide and direct us and that You would keep and protect this place. In Your holy name for nothing else.*

*Oh God of heaven and earth....*

*Hear our prayer and our supplications that we make unto You, Jesus Christ Almighty.*

*Sanctify this place, Lord. Sanctify this congregation.*

*Lord, bless and anoint, and keep the instruments, and the Bibles, and the people, Lord, in your name.*

*Let nothing be done around here but what is in Your Name.*

*Let Your name be on everything!*

*Let Your name be on the Bible!*

*Let Your name be on the songbooks!*

*Let Your name be on this building.*

*And let Your fear... let Your fear be
around this building.*

*And I pray, dear Lord, that You would
keep this in Your name, That Your
name may be here and nothing will
ever be preached here but the truth.
And the truth shall stand!*

*And we pray, Lord, when time shall
come and a one-world ruler shall
stand and rule the world, we pray that
You would protect this place. Amen!*

*That Michael the great prince would
stand up and protect this place
and that all the people that want to
worship You can come inside and
be saved.*

*In Your Holy Name... We ask it, Jesus,
In Your name and we will ever give
You the praise.*

Two years and nine months later, the
intrepid, veteran warrior laid his armor down
and departed to be with the One who was the
Captain of his soul.

Roy, "Popsey" Gibson had been in a coma for three days. Eulah, Vesta Layne, Nara Lee, and Anthony were keeping vigil at his bedside, knowing that there were only hours remaining in his lengthy, productive life.

Nara Lee's son Michael was flying in from Los Angeles, California and she left for a brief time to prepare for his arrival. Vesta Layne and Anthony were at his bedside when suddenly, from the depths of his stomach a ball, as it were, began to move slowly but surely toward his throat. As they watched in amazement, when the mass reached his throat, his eyes opened and a big smile came on his face.

Not until his spirit departed was death able to claim the prophet's body. Vesta Layne said she watched his soul—which appeared as a vapor—exit the room toward the eastern sky.

Roy had preached many times from St. John 7:38, 39:

> *"He that believeth on me as the scripture hath said, out of his belly shall flow rivers of living water." " but this spake he of the Spirit which they that believe on him should receive…*

That spirit in Roy, which Jesus likened to "rivers of living water," returned to the One who gave it.

A CHILD OF ANOTHER CENTURY, SON OF A TIMELESS GOD, THE PROPHET NAMED GIBSON. NOT A MAVERICK, BUT A PIONEER; NEVER A SLOTHFUL SERVANT, BUT ALWAYS A FLAMING EVANGEL. HIS WORKPLACE WAS THE PRIMITIVE BRUSH ARBOR, HIS PRODUCT A LIFE-CHANGING NAME. IF PLACES LIKE HUNTINGTON, LUFKIN, ZAVALLA, STUMPVILLE, OAK FLAT, AND ORA MEANT NOTHING TO MANY, THE SAME CROWD WOULD HAVE AVOIDED HAMLETS LIKE BEHTLEHEM, NAZARETH, AND CAPERNAUM.

DAY AFTER DAY, SOUL AFTER SOUL, HE LABORED ON ACRES CONSIDERED "HARDSCRABBLE" BY MANY. WITH EULAH AT HIS SIDE, AND NONA, VESTA LAYNE, NARA LEE, R.D., AND CLIBBORN IN TOW, TO USE HIS WORDS, "SOMETHING IN HIM JUST WANTED TO GO ON." HE LIVED TO PREACH, EVEN IF IT MEANT ONLY BREAD AND WATER TO EAT AND KHAKI CLOTHES

TO WEAR. THE MESSAGE, THE MISSION WERE EVERYTHING TO HIM. BE HE EVANGELIST OR PASTOR, IT WAS ALWAYS THE TELLING AND RETELLING OF SALVATION'S CHRONICLE.

AS THE SHADOWS LENGTHENED, THE CHURCH WAS REPLACED BY A FEW ROOMS ON PROSPECT STREET IN ALEXANDRIA, LOUISIANA. THE COUCH OR KITCHEN TABLE BECAME HIS PULPIT. BUT WHETHER HE WAS PRAYING FOR THE SICK, ANOINTING A HANDKERCHIEF, OR BONDING A MARRIAGE, THE MESSAGE WAS NEVER DILUTED OR REPLACED. ALONG WITH COFFEE AND GINGER SNAPS, THERE WAS ALWAYS A GENEROUS SERVING OF "NEITHER IS THERE SALVATION IN ANY OTHER…."

AND SO, TIME CLAIMS HIM, THE "ONE GOD" TAKES HIM TO HIS BOSOM. THE NEXT TOWN? IT'S CALLED "NEW JERUSALEM." BLAZE THE TRAIL, POPSEY. WE'LL FOLLOW.

Written by Phil Jones for the cover of Royal Denver "Popsey" Gibson's Funeral Program—used by permission.

# A Tribute to My Mother— Eulah Annie Hudiburgh

Of all the women who were named and profiled in the Bible, only three were described as "beautiful." One more was described as "having a beautiful countenance."

If the Bible were being written today, there is no doubt that Eulah Annie Hudiburgh, wife of Royal Denver Gibson, would be included in that diminutive, highly notable group.

Eulah embraced her roles as wife, mother and then pastor's wife with dignity, aplomb, and mastery. Those who were fortunate enough to dine at her table will never forget the wonderful pastries, succulent fried chicken, and the delicious vegetables and cornbread served often. And did I mention her chicken and dumplings? The list of her culinary delights goes on and on.

But cook and hostess extraordinaire were only a small part of who she was as a person. Among her remarkable gifts was her God-given musical ability. With songbook in hand Eulah would lead the congregation in a lively chorus or hymn while keeping the beat by hitting her songbook with her hand. By the time Nara Lee and Vesta Layne were three and six years old, respectively, Eulah trained them to harmonize with her on such songs as: "No Tears in Heaven." When she was ninety years of age, Eulah joined Nara Lee, Vesta Layne, Murrell Ewing, and others at the Louisiana camp meeting in a rousing rendition of the beloved song, "I'll Have a New Body." The performance brought the entire audience to its feet.

A child of destiny, Eulah and her twin brother Eulon, were half-orphaned by the death of their mother when they were only three months old. Shortly thereafter an adult relative came to visit the twins and exposed them to the highly contagious disease, whooping cough. Eulah was weaker than her brother and the doctor told the twins' caretakers to give all their attention to the boy because the girl was going to die anyway. To the surprise of everyone, Eulah kept on living but her brother, sadly, did not survive. Eulah often lamented the fact that she never got to know her brother.

When Roy made the decision to answer the "call" from God to preach, Eulah supported him fully. She knew that hardship would be a big part of her life, but she met every move and every challenge with enthusiasm, courage, and determination.

Whether she was in her kitchen creating a scrumptious meal, leading the congregation in an inspirational hymn or in a prayer room teaching others to pray by being an example of a powerful prayer warrior she was in her element.

The lessons she deposited in each of her children were far more valuable than any trust fund deposited in a financial institution.

Those who were fortunate enough to have met Eulah and to have spent time with her will never forget the spiritual and material lessons she so unwittingly imparted to them.

So Momsy, please have some chicken and dumplings, perhaps some trays of fried apple and apricot pies and just maybe a banana pudding on the menu at the "Marriage Supper of the Lamb." The angels and I would love that!

Adoringly,
The Author

# ABOUT THE AUTHOR

Nara Gibson Wenrich was born in Huntington, Texas and attended elementary schools in Huntington, Zavalla, and Lufkin, Texas. She graduated from French high school in Beaumont Texas and continued her education at Louisiana State University at Alexandria and at Louisiana College in Pineville, Louisiana.

Nara is best known for her service as church and choir pianist for many churches beginning at her father's church in Lufkin Texas at the age of ten. She continues to be involved in ministry at her local church by speaking and playing the piano occasionally.

Although this is her first published book, Nara has had articles and profiles published in various Christian publications.

Nara moved to Dallas Texas in 1990 to be near her daughter, Marla Savant-Box, son-in law Douglas Box, and her twin grandchildren Audrey Camille Box and Dalton Cloyce Box.

**Intermedia
Publishing Group**
*Publishing That Works For You*

## Do you need a speaker?

Whether you want to purchase bulk copies of *Royal Denver Gibson* or buy another book for a friend, get it now at: www.imprbooks.com.

Do you want Nara Gibson Wenrich to speak to your group or event? Then contact Larry Davis at: (623) 337-8710 or email: ldavis@intermediapr.com or use the contact form at: www.intermediapr.com.

For your publishing needs, contact Terry Whalin, Publisher, at Intermedia Publishing Group, (623) 337-8710 or email: twhalin@intermediapub.com or use the contact form at: www.intermediapub.com.